The
50 WRITING PROMPTS
WORKBOOK
for Your 3rd Grader

by Linda Chiara

Copyright © 2023 by Linda Chiara
All rights reserved.
No portion of this book may be reproduced in any form without written permission from the publisher or author, except as permitted by U.S. copyright law.

This Writing Prompts

Workbook

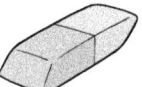

Belongs to

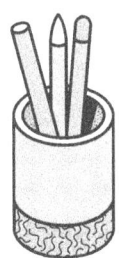

Writing prompt 1

Date : _____

Pretend you're a snowflake falling to the ground. Write about all your adventures from the moment you start swirling in the air until the moment you finally melt away.

Writing prompt 1

Writing prompt 2

Date: _____

Describe your favorite candy without saying the name of the candy.

Writing prompt 2

Writing prompt 3

Date: _____

Close your eyes for a few seconds and then open them. What is the first thing you see? Write a paragraph describing it.

Writing prompt 3

Writing prompt 4

Date: _____

You are invited to a pizza party. But to your surprise, the pizza has hot fudge sauce as a topping.

Will you try it? Do you think you will like it?

Writing prompt 4

 # Writing prompt 5

Date : _____

Lucky you! You've won a trip to Mars. However, you can only take three special things with you. What things will you take and why are you choosing them?

Writing prompt 5

# Writing prompt 6

Date: _____

Write a story about your favorite thing to do on a rainy day.

Writing prompt 6

Writing prompt 7

Date: _____

Is there anything you can do with your thumb that you can't do with your pinkie finger? Explain with examples.

Writing prompt 7

 # Writing prompt 8

Date: _____

Write about something that made you laugh today.

Writing prompt 8

Writing prompt 9

Date: _____

Write a story about a magical rainbow that leads to a treasure.

Writing prompt 9

Writing prompt 10

Date : _____

What would you do if you could breathe fire like a dragon?

Writing prompt 10

Writing prompt 11

Date: _____

Your Uncle Jimmy is famous for the silly gifts he gives on birthdays. Today is your birthday and he really outdid himself. You couldn't believe your eyes when you opened your birthday present and saw a ___! Describe what Uncle Jimmy gave you.

Writing prompt 11

Writing prompt 12

Date: _____

A spaceship has landed in your backyard. Describe the alien that steps off the ship and what you do when he approaches.

Writing prompt 12

Writing prompt 13

Date: _____

If you could pick just one toy to play with every day for one month, what toy would that be?

Writing prompt 13

Writing prompt 14

Date : _____

Explain how a violin sounds to someone who is deaf.

Writing prompt 14

Writing prompt 15

Date : _____

When you woke up this morning you discovered you were in your dog's bed on the floor and he was snoring in your bed with his head on the pillow! What do you think happened in the night to make you two change places?

Writing prompt 15

Writing prompt 16

Date: _____

Everything you touch today turns to gold. Is that a good thing or a bad thing? What will you do when it is time to eat your lunch?

Writing prompt 16

Writing prompt 17

Date : _____

Have you ever had goosebumps? What does it mean when you get goosebumps?

_____
_____
_____
_____
_____
_____
_____
_____
_____
_____
_____
_____
_____

Writing prompt 17

Writing prompt 18

Date: _____

Write a poem and include these words in it: flop, pop, hop, top, mop, shop, stop.

Writing prompt 18

Writing prompt 19

Date: _____

Write a story that starts with the line "I used to think I wasn't very smart" and that ends with the line "And that's why I'm the smartest person in the world".

Writing prompt 19

Writing prompt 20

Date: _____

What is your favorite thing in your bedroom that isn't your bed? And why do you like it?

Writing prompt 20

Writing prompt 21

Date : _____

What is your favorite ride at an amusement park? Why do you like it so much?

Writing prompt 21

Writing prompt 22

Date: _____

Name three things that you can't buy with money that mean more to you than the things you can buy.

Writing prompt 22

Writing prompt 23

Date: _____

Write a story and use these words in it: twinkle, rabbit, hiccup and basketball.

Writing prompt 23

Writing prompt 24

Date: _____

Today is mixed up food day. The spaghetti sauce is blue, your banana is pink, both inside and out, and your apple is black! Would you be able to enjoy these foods if they were these colors? Why or why not?

Writing prompt 24

Writing prompt 25

Date: _____

Today you're a candle on a birthday cake. Describe your day.

Writing prompt 25

Writing prompt 26

Date: _____

Most people like to put mustard on their hotdogs, but you prefer to put grape jelly on them. Explain why that is.

Writing prompt 26

Writing prompt 27

Date: _____

What is the most difficult thing about being a kid? What is the best part?

Writing prompt 27

Writing prompt 28

Date: _____

You have been given the chance to be invisible for a day. What is the first place you go and what do you do when you get there?

Writing prompt 28

Writing prompt 29

Date :

This morning when you woke up it was raining. However, it wasn't raining water. Instead gummy bears were falling down from the sky. Write a story called, "The Day It Rained Gummy Bears".

Writing prompt 29

Writing prompt 30

Date: _____

It's the first day of school and when your teacher walks into class, she has all of her clothes on backwards. Even her shoes on are the wrong feet! What do you think is going on?

Writing prompt 30

Writing prompt 31

Date : _____

You woke up this morning and discovered that you have lost your ability to smell. You can't smell stinky things, which is good; but you also can't smell great things like flowers or your mother's perfume. What smell do you think you will miss the most and why?

_____
_____
_____
_____
_____
_____
_____
_____
_____
_____

Writing prompt 31

Writing prompt 32

Date: _____

Describe your best friend using three words. Why did you choose those words?

Writing prompt 32

Writing prompt 33

Date: _____

Write a story using these words: airplane, mayonnaise, pencil and bathing suit.

Writing prompt 33

Writing prompt 34

Date: _____

You are a candy bar on the shelf in the grocery store. Someone has just put you into their cart.

Think about what other items might be in the cart with you. Write a story about your adventure.

Writing prompt 34

 # Writing prompt 35

Date : _____

Your school's lunch menu says Thursday's lunch will be a surprise. You like surprises, but you never expected to see this on your lunch tray! What was the surprise lunch?

Writing prompt 35

Writing prompt 36

Date: _____

Describe what you think a bird thinks about when she's sitting in her nest.

Writing prompt 36

Writing prompt 37

Date: _____

It's the first day of summer vacation and you've already broken your leg! What kind of summer do you think you will have?

Writing prompt 37

Writing prompt 38

Date : _____

Pick someone in your family and describe them in detail.

Writing prompt 38

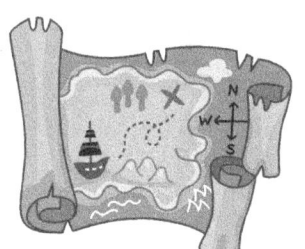 # Writing prompt 39

Date: _____

<u>You've discovered a treasure map in an old library book. What do you think the treasure is and where is it located?</u>

Writing prompt 39

Writing prompt 40

Date : _____

What is your absolute favorite dessert and why?

_____

_____

_____

_____

_____

_____

_____

_____

_____

_____

_____

_____

_____

_____

_____

Writing prompt 40

Writing prompt 41

Date: _____

What is something that you have done recently for the very first time?

Writing prompt 41

Writing prompt 42

Date: _____

You just discovered a magic tree in your neighborhood. What are three wishes you would wish for?

Writing prompt 42

 # Writing prompt 43

Date: _____

Write a story about an amazing creature that lives under the sea.

Writing prompt 43

Writing prompt 44

Date : _____

Do you prefer to read a scary story that gives you goosebumps or a book that is silly and makes you laugh? Why did you choose the one you did?

Writing prompt 44

 # Writing prompt 45

Date: _____

What is the one ride at an amusement park that you don't ever want to go on? Why do you feel that way?

Writing prompt 45

 # Writing prompt 46

Date : _____

You went on a picnic with your family and someone forgot to close the car windows. Now there are bears in the car! How would you get them out?

Writing prompt 46

Writing prompt 47

Date : _____

Would you prefer to be a big, beautiful shade tree or a small, colorful, sweet smelling rose? Explain why you picked the one you did.

Writing prompt 47

Writing prompt 48

Date : _____

What family rule do you have to follow that you think is unfair?

Writing prompt 48

 # Writing prompt 49

Date : _____

You found an unusual ring in an antique shop. What happens when you wear it?

Writing prompt 49

Writing prompt 50

Date: _____

Where is your favorite place to go with your family? Is it a movie, a park, a restaurant or something else? Write about it.

Writing prompt 50

www.ingramcontent.com/pod-product-compliance
Lightning Source LLC
Chambersburg PA
CBHW080747060526
44119CB00073B/182